AF265376

The Pocket Book
of
CONFIDENCE

by
A Pocket Full of Happiness

Table of Contents

How this book works

You pick what you do or don't do. I don't mind, I promise.

You can skip parts or repeat parts as much as you want. Do whatever is useful for you.

Be kind to yourself, some of this is intense and deep - take breaks.

You can go back to front, or pick a random page. This is not a novel. Go in any order.

Wreck this book, scribble, draw, journal, rip out a page or two, take it for a walk in the rain, use this book as you please.

Chapter 1

About me

A little info about me. I'm Louie, I'm a coach and writer of novels and now this coaching book. My self-confidence was the bane of my existence - it still is sometimes on bad days, but now I've learnt how to manage it, and work with my brain to do the things I want to do.

This book is what I needed when I was sixteen, and eighteen, and twenty, and twenty two... and so I hope this book helps you, because the methods used in it helped me over the last few years.

It is a **self-guided** book, so when things feel a little too deep or hard, you can skip them, or stop and have a break. You set the pace. You pick what you do or don't do. For me, I found that it felt that sometimes there was no right answer to the questions I was being asked by my coach or therapist. **I've discovered that there isn't a right answer.**

There is what your gut is telling you is right, what your friends say, what your parents say, what your culture says, what your upbringing says, what the demons in your head say, and finally what you say...

For now, any answer is okay, there might be multiple answers - there often is. They are all answers - you get to decide what you listen to. Either way, write them all down, and you can come back to the book and deicide what you want to do later on.

You don't have to make any conclusions right now. But at least you have a log of what you were once thinking.

In my own experience, I've found that my self-confidence displays itself in many visible and not-so-visible ways. Including negative self-talk in my own head, deprecating jokes to my friends and family, and a feeling of impostor syndrome.

It isn't just the feeling of 'I'm not brave today', for me it's a sense of guilt for taking up space in the world. Coaching can help you look past that and work it all out - how to deal with it, and how to get on with things around your confidence.

I'm learning to drive and I'm realising my car has every right to be on the road as anyone else's does. **You have every right to be strong and confident and brave and wonderful.**

When you look at what motivates you, or what drives you it is easier to be confident. It's not just a presentation in a stressful setting, it's an opportunity to show what you know to people. It changes from a terrifying driving test into the first step in getting your freedom.

This book should help you find your motivators and drivers – to help you reframe the things knocking you down into opportunities you can't wait to overcome.

This book should help you understand why your brain is 'being mean' (it's normally because whatever you're doing is scary and brains like to try and keep us safe). When you understand why your brain is being weird and negative – you can remind it that you're in control and everything is going to be okay.

Chapter 2

Why I believe in coaching

Once I asked for help after failing 2nd year of university, things got better.

I met my wonderful coach Beth, and she helped me turn my life around. She helped me to plan around my anxiety, she asked all the questions that dug into my psyche and helped me understand what was holding me back and what to do about it.

I thought logically (instead of anxiously), connected with others, worked with my anxiety (not against it), took my time, held space for myself to feel better, was kind to myself, and took back the reins to my life all through coaching.

I trained to become a coach in 2023 and felt everything click into place - coaching was what I was made for.

Coaching isn't therapy. I can't fix you.

Coaching can be therapeutic. It can be cathartic, and revelatory. If you let it be.

Coaching can help you plan around your mental health, it can help you understand yourself better.

Coaching can help you work out what is holding you back with your confidence. Coaching can help you regain some control over your big feelings and big emotions.

Coaching can help you work out what drives and motivates you - which can help you find reasons to do things that once scared you.

Coaching can change your life.

Now, if what you need is a therapist, or counselling - go ahead and talk to your GP. Coaching can't fix mental health.

This book can help you gain confidence to talk to people about getting help, and it can help reframe some of the spiders in the closet. But it is not going to help you turn on the light and look at the cobwebs you've accumulated in your life.

Therapy is very helpful - I've had lots of it. And coaching is very helpful, I've had lots of that too... but they are different. And I am not a mental health professional, no matter how much lived experience I have.

Chapter 3

Guided journalling
with coaching
questions

How this section works:

You can take a question and mull it over each day, or you can sit down and do them all in one sitting with a cup of tea. Or you can take them and write them on a post-it to think about through a week. You can do whatever you want with these questions.

I have left you some lined pages to write what you want, there are also some blank pages to draw, or doodle, or mindmap, or scribble whatever comes up.

It's up to you.

You can do them in any order, in no order, or at random - whatever feels right. Each page has a letter so you can answer the questions like: C3, A10, B4. There is more spare pages after E (p38) or after p81 so enjoy the space or lines to do what you want!

1. What's on your mind?

2. Why did you pick up this book?

3. What scares you the most?

4. What's holding you back?

5. What is your inner voice saying?

6. What do you want your inner voice to say?

7. Are you a critic or a cheerleeder to yourself?

8. What do you need to hear from someone?

9. What do you wish someone said to you?

10. What can you remind yourself of that makes you happy?

11. What are you avoiding?

12. What is one small step in the right direction?

1. What are your highest dreams?

2. What do you need to do to take one step towards your dreams?

3. What do you want to do with your life?

4. What do you need to step away from to help you be more confident?

5. What can you tell yourself as you take brave steps?

6. What do you feel you should be doing?

7. What do you want to do right now?

8. What can you celebrate about yourself right now, regardless of how small it may seem?

9. If you could give yourself permission to be confident, what would you say to yourself?

1. What are the barriers stopping you from feeling fully confident, and what could you do to address one of them?

2. How does comparing yourself to others impact your confidence? What might help you to focus more on your own growth?

3. What's one skill or talent you've always wanted to develop, but haven't due to lack of confidence?

4. What are some things you do regularly that make you feel good about yourself?

5. What are some situations where you tend to doubt yourself? What do you think drives that doubt?

1. What areas of your life do you feel most confident in, and why do you think that is?

2. What specific beliefs do you hold about yourself that affect your confidence?

3. If you felt more confident, how would your day-to-day life change?

4. What are some of the qualities or skills you admire in others that you'd like to develop in yourself?

5. What would happen if you were less critical of yourself and more accepting? How might that affect your confidence?

6. What does confidence mean to you personally?

1. Who is someone who can help you?

2. What has helped you feel better in the past?

3. What obstacles can you get rid of?

4. What can help you in the future?

5. What's one belief about yourself you'd like to challenge or change to feel more confident?

6. Can you describe a time when you felt truly confident? What factors contributed to that feeling?

7. Who in your life has supported or encouraged your confidence? How did they do that?

8. What are some small actions you can take today to feel more confident in yourself?

Chapter 4

Exercises and practical steps to confidence

How this section works:

These exercises are based on helping you think outside-the-box or in creative ways to help you understand things in a different way.

I have given you an example of how to lay out the exercise or complete it on paper / in the book, but feel free to use a big notebook, computer/tablet, or chalk on concrete to get these done.

Ultimately do what feels right, but I recommend giving each of them a go.

Two of these exercises have youtube videos that can teach you how to do them, or to give you better context - so I point you to those for better understanding but they are not 100% crucial.

Exercise 1 = Values and Motivators

This exercise helps you to find what drives you - this can help push you to do something because, *even if your confidence says no,* you are driven to do it.

If you understand *why* something is important it can take the pressure off something that seems daunting.

My driving test is coming up soon, and I'm nervous - which means my self-confidence is low. I keep thinking of the pressure that comes with the test. If I fail, I can't drive alone, and if I can't drive alone I have no freedom.

So what motivates me to do well in my driving test? *Freedom.*

How can I reframe the test to help me to have more confidence?

Logically, I know that I've had hours and hours of driving lessons, I know that I can do all the parking manoeuvres, I know that my parents trust me, I know that I trust myself to make good choices when I drive.

If I take a deep breath and think rationally about the test, I know I'm going to be bored of driving around the same miles of Northampton roads by January - I know I'm going to be *so* ready to drive alone and blast my crappy taste in music without a parent sat next to me ...

I know that I'm ready for my test. I have confidence that I'll be fine.

Think about some specific scenarios that you're nervous about and that your self-confidence seems to be dwindling on... see if you can reframe them and think logically about them.

What do you know? What is the truth, rather than focusing on the what-if's and the doubts.

What can you control? What can you do about the things you can't? If you can't control them - then that's not your fault.

For me, the driver and motivator of passing my test is the ability to go anywhere I want, whenever I want. It's freedom and self-sufficiency. Think about why the scenario is important, what is the reason behind wanting to get it done? What will it mean to you when you do get it done? What do you get out of it when it's finished?

Exercise 2 = The Power of Words

Watch = *The Power of Words Speech - by Mohammed Qahtani (Youtube channel: English Speeches)*

This speech taught me how important the words we use are. I realised that the constant degrading I was doing to myself in my head wasn't helping. This speech let me see how powerful those self-reminders were. I highly reccomend watching it and exploring what words you are using to yourself.

A good way of reframing those words are to see if you would use those words to your best-friend, siblings, or grandparents.

I kept telling myself to 'shut up', and I was constantly making myself the butt of jokes. If I think about doing the same to my brother, telling him that he is 'useless' or that he is an 'idiot' constantly *as I do to myself* - I wouldn't expect him to like me much.

So why did I see it as normal for my brain to be saying that to me everyday?

Have an explore of what you're saying to yourself and what you think that's doing to your self-confidence.

Exercise 3 = Power Poses

Watch = *Your Body Language May Shape Who You Are - By Amy Cuddy (Youtube channel: TED)*

Imagine you have a big meeting with a boss, or important person. You're waiting outside their office to be called in, you're not sure why you're there but you know it's important.

Your palms are sweaty, you're hot and flustered, you're fidgety and nervous.

Do you...

A: Sit there and sweat until you're an anxious puddle of a human, slouched in on itself and barely taking up space, too scared and confused to make a single valid point when you get summoned into that room?

OR

B: Stand up, shake off the jitters, take some deep breaths, centre yourself and calm yourself down, muster up your strength. Sit back down and breathe deeply, posture tall and strong - and wait cooly to be invited in, ready for whatever you're about to face?

Which version do you think will have the better outcome? Which version of you will come off stronger and more powerful? Which version of you appears to have more confidence?

Sometimes it's about faking it until you make it. You read other people's body language everyday - some people look nervous, or tense, or happy, or tired...

Your brain reads your body language too - so even if you can't control your nerves, you can control your breathing and your body's movements to be calmer and more confident.

Sometimes you have to pretend to be cool, calm and collected to become cool, calm and collected. Sometimes you end up feeling more confident because you are more in control of your body and how you present yourself.

Take a moment to breathe calmly and think about your body language and how you can use it to your advantage. Think about what small thing you can implement into your day to make you feel a little stronger.

I like to press my feet firmly into the floor - it helps me feel strong and puts my nervous energy somewhere. Nobody knows. Nobody sees a difference. I also breathe slowly to stop hyperventilating and panicking more.

But try it. Can you have bad posture with your feet firmly on the floor? (if you say yes you're lying, and you look like you're straining for a poop).

Try and draw yourself (stick figures will do) in power poses. Try and draw you looking confident and happy. Try and draw yourself looking like a superhero.

Now tell me how that feels, and what you're going to implement today.

Exercise 4 = Looks can be deceiving

Have you ever seen someone on the street, or in a shop and thought, "wow they're amazing!" You know nothing about them other than the fact that they dress cool, or have a great hair-do, or have a style that you love.

1. What does a cool person look like to you?
2. What does a confident person look like to you?
3. What does a calm person look like to you?
4. What have you got in your wardrobe that makes you feel epic?
5. What have you got in your closets that makes you look amazing?
6. What do you need to have to make you feel calm?
7. What is stopping you from piling all those things onto your body right now?

Try and imagine what you'd look like with those things added to you. Maybe a new haircut is what would make you feel ace, or maybe a cool new jacket or your old shoes you wore once when you had that amazing job.

Draw a stick-figure or simply draw them all out to see what you need to go and find for your ultimate new look.

How does that feel? What's different?

Congratulations!

You've finished the Pocket Book of Confidence.

I hope it helped you. There are plenty more pages after this one for you to write out your findings and draw/doodle your way to more confidence.

If you want to find out more about the Pocket Books Series, look to the @pocket.of.happiness Instagram page for lots of updates.

The next few books will be based on Communication, Time Management, and Burn-out.

Good luck out there!

Love, Louie <3